It all seems to have happened so long ago.

The train must have traveled for many miles, for

many years. Or maybe it was only for a few minutes.

During my journey I witnessed many events,

and imagined many others in the pages of my diary.

I am an old man now, but my dreams continue to

travel, far beyond the edge of that last cliff.

Text and illustrations ©1993 Guy Billout

Jacket designed by Rita Marshall

Published in 1993 by Creative Editions,

123 South Broad Street, Mankato, Minnesota 56001 USA

Creative Editions is an imprint of Creative Education, Inc.

The publication of this book is a joint venture between
Creative Education, Inc. and American Education Publishing.

Library of Congress Cataloging-in-Publication Data

Billout, Guy. Journey/illustrated by Guy Billout.

Summary: Illustrations without words depict scenes out of a train
window as the train moves through the countryside – and through time.

ISBN 1-56846-081-3   Printed in Italy.

(1. Stories without words. 2. Railroads-Trains-Fiction.) I. Title.

PZ7.B4997Jo   1993   93-17094

(E) – dc20   CIP

JOURNEY

·TRAVEL·DIARY·OF·A·DAYDREAMER·

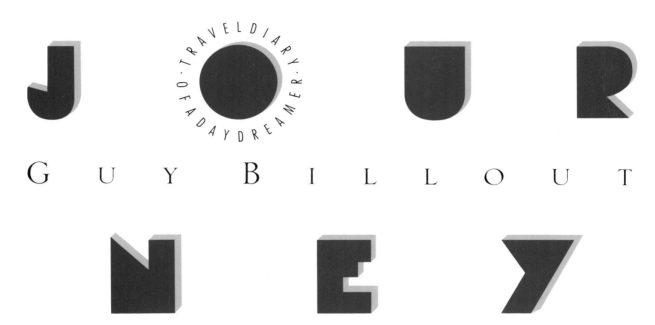

GUY BILLOUT

CREATIVE EDITIONS

Mankato

June 12, the 10:40 train

December, or maybe it was August

Garden in May

August 13, a blue moon

July 17, heavy rain

October 12, 23° 09′ North Latitude 73° 29′ 13″ West Longitude

April 14, one and a half miles deep

February 22, steps

July 12, exit

June 8, estuary

Sunday afternoon in September

August, 102° in the shade

January 30, midnight

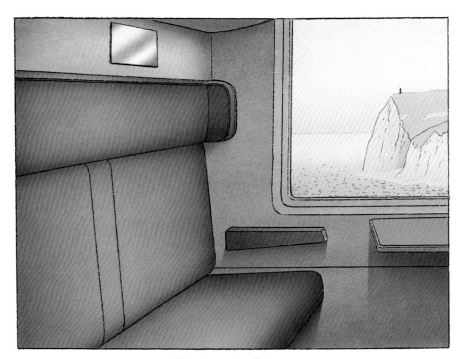

March 11, the Atlantic